Junior Drug Awareness

Ecstasy
& Other
Designer Drugs

Junior Drug Awareness

Junior Drug Awareness

Ecstasy
& Other
Designer Drugs

Introduction by **BARRY R. McCAFFREY**
Director, Office of National Drug Control Policy

Foreword by **STEVEN L. JAFFE, M.D.**
Senior Consulting Editor,
Professor of Child and Adolescent Psychiatry, Emory University

Kristine Brennan

Chelsea House Publishers
Philadelphia

CHELSEA HOUSE PUBLISHERS
Editor in Chief Stephen Reginald
Production Manager Pamela Loos
Director of Photography Judy L. Hasday
Art Director Sara Davis
Managing Editor James D. Gallagher
Senior Production Editor LeeAnne Gelletly

Staff for ECSTASY AND OTHER DESIGNER DRUGS
Senior Editor Therese De Angelis
Associate Art Director Takeshi Takahashi
Cover Illustrator/Designer Keith Trego
Editorial Assistant Jessica Carey
Produced by 21st Century Publishing and Communications, Inc.

Cover Photo © Roy Morsch/The Stock Market

The Chelsea House World Wide Website address is http://www.chelseahouse.com

First Printing
1 3 5 7 9 8 6 4 2

Library of Congress Cataloging-in-Publication Data
Brennan, Kristine, 1969–
Ecstasy and other designer drugs/Kristine Brennan.
80 pp.   cm. — (Junior drug awareness series)
Includes bibliographical references and index.
Summary: Describes the history, origins, effects, and dangers of such designer drugs as Ecstasy, PCP, and fentanyl analogs.
ISBN 0-7910-5201-X (hc)
1. MDMA (Drug)—Juvenile literature. 2. Designer drugs—Juvenile literature. [1. Designer drugs. 2. Drugs. 3. Drug abuse.] I. Title. II. Series: Junior drug awareness.
HV5822.M38B74   1999
362.29'9—dc21   99-22425
                                                          CIP

CONTENTS

by Barry R. McCaffrey
Director, Office of National
Drug Control Policy

Staying Away from Illegal Drugs, Tobacco Products, and Alcohol

Good health allows you to be as strong, happy, smart, and skillful as you can possibly be. The worst thing about illegal drugs is that they damage people from the inside. Our bodies and minds are wonderful, complicated systems that run like finely tuned machines when we take care of ourselves.

Doctors prescribe legal drugs, called medicines, to heal us when we become sick, but dangerous chemicals that are not recommended by doctors, nurses, or pharmacists are called illegal drugs. These drugs cannot be bought in stores because they harm different organs of the body, causing illness or even death. Illegal drugs, such as marijuana, cocaine or "crack," heroin, methamphetamine ("meth"), and other dangerous substances are against the law because they affect our ability to think, work, play, sleep, or eat.

If anyone ever offers you illegal drugs or any kind of pills, liquids, substances to smoke, or shots to inject into your body, tell them you're not interested. You should report drug pushers—people who distribute these poisons—to parents, teachers, police, coaches, clergy, or other adults whom you trust.

Cigarettes and alcohol are also illegal for youngsters. Tobacco products and drinks like wine, beer, and liquor are particularly harmful for children and teenagers because their bodies, especially their nervous systems, are still developing. For this reason, young people are more likely to be hurt by illicit drugs—including cigarettes and alcohol. These two products kill more people—from cancer, and automobile accidents caused by intoxicated drivers—than all other drugs combined. We say about drug use: "Users are losers." Be a winner and stay away from illegal drugs, tobacco products, and alcoholic beverages.

Here are four reasons why you shouldn't use illegal drugs:

- Illegal drugs can cause brain damage.
- Illegal drugs are "psychoactive." This means that they change your personality or the way you feel. They also impair your judgment. While under the influence of drugs, you are more likely to endanger your life or someone else's. You will also be less able to protect yourself from danger.
- Many illegal drugs are addictive, which means that once a person starts taking them, stopping is extremely difficult. An addict's body craves the drug and becomes dependent upon it. The illegal drug–user may become sick if the drug is discontinued and so may become a slave to drugs.

- Some drugs, called "gateway" substances, can lead a person to take more-dangerous drugs. For example, a 12-year-old who smokes marijuana is 79 times more likely to have an addiction problem later in life than a child who never tries marijuana.

Here are some reasons why you shouldn't drink alcoholic beverages, including beer and wine coolers:

- Alcohol is the second leading cause of death in our country. More than 100,000 people die every year because of drinking.
- Adolescents are twice as likely as adults to be involved in fatal alcohol-related car crashes.
- Half of all assaults against girls or women involve alcohol.
- Drinking is illegal if you are under the age of 21. You could be arrested for this crime.

Here are three reasons why you shouldn't smoke cigarettes:

- Nicotine is highly addictive. Once you start smoking, it is very hard to stop, and smoking cigarettes causes lung cancer and other diseases. Tobacco- and nicotine-related diseases kill more than 400,000 people every year.
- Each day, 3,000 kids begin smoking. One-third of these youngsters will probably have their lives shortened because of tobacco use.
- Children who smoke cigarettes are almost six times more likely to use other illegal drugs than kids who don't smoke.

If your parents haven't told you how they feel about the dangers of illegal drugs, ask them. One of every 10 kids aged 12 to 17 is using illegal drugs. They do not understand the risks they are taking with their health and their lives. However, the vast majority of young people in America are smart enough to figure out that drugs, cigarettes, and alcohol could rob them of their future. Be your body's best friend: guard your mental and physical health by staying away from drugs.

WHY SHOULD I LEARN ABOUT DRUGS?

**Steven L. Jaffe, M.D., Senior Consulting Editor,
Professor of Child and Adolescent Psychiatry,
Emory University**

Your grandparents and great-grandparents did not think much about "drug awareness." That's because drugs, to most of them, simply meant "medicine."

Of the three types of drugs, medicine is the good type. Medicines such as penicillin and aspirin promote healing and help sick people get better.

Another type of drug is obviously bad for you because it is poison. Then there are the kinds of drugs that fool you, such as marijuana and LSD. They make you feel good, but they harm your body and brain.

Our great crisis today is that this third category of drugs has become widely abused. Drugs of abuse are everywhere, not just in rough neighborhoods. Many teens are introduced to drugs by older brothers, sisters, friends, or even friends' parents. Some people may use only a little bit of a drug, but others who inherited a tendency to become addicted may move on to using drugs all the time. If a family member is or was an alcoholic or an addict, a young person is at greater risk of becoming one.

Drug abuse can weaken us physically. Worse, it can cause

permanent mental damage. Our brain is the most important part of our body. Our thoughts, hopes, wishes, feelings, and memories are located there, within 100 billion nerve cells. Alcohol and drugs that are abused will harm—and even destroy—these cells. During the teen years, your brain continues to develop and grow, but drugs and alcohol can impair this growth.

I treat all types of teenagers at my hospital programs and in my office. Many suffer from depression or anxiety. A lot of them abuse drugs and alcohol, and this makes their depression or fears worse. I have celebrated birthdays and high school graduations with many of my patients. But I have also been to sad funerals for others who have died from problems with drug abuse.

Doctors understand more about drugs today than ever before. We've learned that some substances (even some foods) that we once thought were harmless can actually cause health problems. And for some people, medicines that help relieve one symptom might cause problems in other ways. This is because each person's body chemistry and immune system are different.

For all of these reasons, drug awareness is important for everyone. We need to learn which drugs to avoid or question—not only the destructive, illegal drugs we hear so much about in the news, but also ordinary medicines we buy at the supermarket or pharmacy. We need to understand that even "good" drugs can hurt us if they are not used correctly. We also need accurate scientific knowledge, not just rumors we hear from other teens.

Drug awareness enables you to make good decisions. It allows you to become powerful and strong and have a meaningful life!

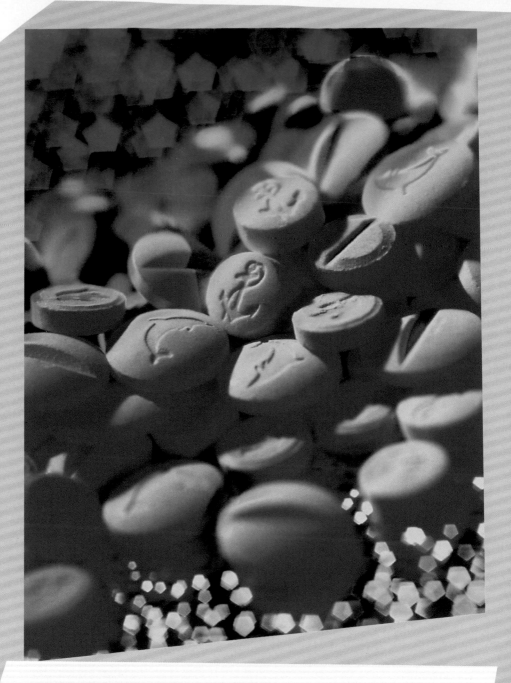

Designer drugs have different chemical ingredients and names. This batch of Ecstasy tablets is stamped with various designs that are supposed to assure users of the pills' quality. But Ecstasy is an illegal drug made by outlaw drugmakers.

DRUGS BY DESIGN

Human beings naturally seek new and pleasurable experiences. If you've ever sat on a swing and twisted up the chains to make it spin, you've attempted to alter the way your senses work. Sometimes, people ingest, smoke, snort, or inject **drugs** to change their sensory perceptions. Some historians believe that Native Americans and Mexicans smoked the leaves of the *Cannabis sativa* plant—**marijuana**—even before Europeans arrived in the Americas. To this day, members of the Native American Church experience visions while consuming parts of the peyote plant during religious ceremonies. Some native South Americans chew the leaves of the coca plant to combat feelings of fatigue and hunger.

There have been many "accidental" drug users throughout history as well. Medieval Europeans who ate bread made from rye flours sometimes became intoxicated by a fungus called ergot that grows on rye. The powerful **hallucinogen** LSD (lysergic acid diethylamide) is made to mimic the effects of ergot. A hallucinogen is a drug that causes people to see, hear, or sense things that aren't really there. When people ate bread baked with ergot-contaminated flour, they experienced this frightening effect. They also felt dizzy and sometimes suffered from gangrene, a disease that kills the body's soft tissues.

At the dawn of the 20th century in the United States, drug use was a part of daily life. It has been reported that in proportion to the population, there were more drug addicts in the United States in 1900 than there are today. That was because so-called patent medicines were easily available. Patent medicines were potions used to treat ailments such as headaches, nervousness, and toothaches—almost any health complaint a person might have. The active ingredients in patent medicines included cocaine, heroin, and morphine.

Drug addicts were not usually considered criminals since the use of patent medicines was legal and commonplace. Public opinion on drugs soon shifted, though. As the number of drug addicts soared, the U.S. government passed laws that placed the use of drugs like morphine under strict legal regulations. By the 1920s, it was illegal to possess such drugs without a prescription. The new laws succeeded in reducing the total number of drug addicts in the United States, but people who were still determined to get their "fix" began to operate outside the law.

During the 1960s, many young people began rejecting the values held by their parents, such as trust in the government and respect for authority. They turned to illegal drugs such as the hallucinogen LSD, or "acid," for pleasure and excitement. Using drugs also had the added "benefit" of shocking and upsetting adults.

By the late 1960s, tough new laws against selling and using LSD were in effect. That didn't stop some people from trying to make acid in their own private laboratories, though. Illegal drugmakers bought their own equipment and ingredients, hoping to make their money back hundreds of times over by selling home-made LSD and other drugs.

Underground drugmakers set up shop in basements, abandoned buildings, or isolated sites to avoid getting caught by police. This crude setup was found in a motel in Oklahoma in 1997. The drug-makers acquired the chemicals to make methamphetamine, or "speed," from ordinary household products such as lighter fluid, Sudafed, foam coffee cups, and lithium batteries.

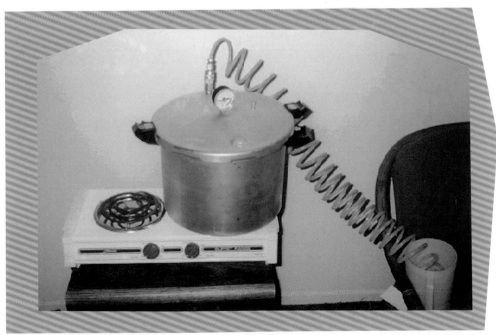

The Origins of Designer Drugs

The underground, or secretive, drug-manufacturing business is the result of years of attempts by illegal chemists to elude authorities. By the early 1980s, the social climate had turned sharply against drug abuse. President Ronald Reagan and his wife, Nancy, launched an anti-drug campaign whose slogan was "Just Say No."

The passage of the Controlled Substances Act of 1970 placed many illegal drugs on a list regulated by the U.S. Drug Enforcement Administration (DEA). In this system, drugs are placed in one of five categories ("schedules") on the basis of strict criteria. The chart on the opposite page shows these categories.

During the Reagan Administration, many drugs were added to the restrictive Schedules I and II, but the underground drugmaking business continued. The skills of outlaw chemists varied widely. Some, however, were every bit as talented as legitimate scientists. Frustrated in their efforts to produce and sell the outlawed big moneymaker drugs such as acid, amphetamines, heroin, and phencyclidine, they came up with a new way to make drugs without technically breaking the law. They started to alter the chemical formulas of Schedule I and II drugs, creating brand-new drugs that have similar effects on the body. These new **analogs,** though closely related to their illegal **parent drugs,** were not yet included in schedules. That meant that for the time being, they were technically legal. A chemist

Schedule I Drugs

(includes heroin, LSD, marijuana)

- Have a high potential for abuse
- Have no recognized medical uses
- Require researchers to get a special government license to make or use them in a legitimate laboratory setting
- Carry prison sentences and fines for unauthorized manufacture, sale, or possession

Schedule II Drugs

(includes meperidine, fentanyl, cocaine, and amphetamines)

- Have a high to moderate potential for abuse
- Are illegal without a doctor's prescription

Schedule III and IV Drugs

(includes selected stimulants and depressants)

- Are less regulated than Schedule I and II drugs
- Are legal with a doctor's prescription

Schedule V Drugs

(includes selected narcotic compounds)

- Are less regulated than Schedule III and IV drugs
- Are considered over-the-counter drugs and are available at pharmacies and drugstores for medicinal purposes

from the University of California at Davis named Garry Henderson was the first person to use the term **designer drugs** to describe these new chemicals that sidestepped U.S. drug laws.

The Reagan Administration responded to the growing problem of designer drugs by pressuring Congress to pass the 1986 Controlled Substances Analogs Act. This law defines an illegal analog drug as any drug whose chemical formula or effect on the body closely resembles that of a drug already included in Schedules I or II.

The new law made the existing designer drugs—as well as most new analogs that underground chemists could cook up—illegal. Unwilling to give up their thriving businesses, however, outlaw drugmakers kept tinkering with the chemical formulas of drugs to create new analogs that were stronger, longer-lasting, and more valuable on the street than previous analogs.

Designer versions of the Schedule II drug fentanyl are good examples of how chemists can dramatically increase a drug's effects with just a few minor changes. Under a doctor's supervision, fentanyl is a powerful pain reliever used during surgery and to ease severe pain in seriously ill patients. This fast-acting drug also produces an intense high. Although fentanyl is many times stronger than the painkiller morphine, a fentanyl high lasts only about half an hour. Designer drugmakers quickly learned how to make the high last for hours by making just a few changes to the fentanyl **molecule**. (A molecule is the smallest unit of a substance.)

Illegal chemists also designed fentanyl analogs to

President Ronald Reagan and First Lady Nancy Reagan coined the slogan "Just Say No" as part of a publicity campaign that warned kids about the dangers of experimenting with drugs.

be even stronger than fentanyl itself. They had to manufacture only a tiny amount to make a lot of money. They could "cut" as little as a tablespoon of superstrong, snowy-white fentanyl analog powder with many pounds of a cheap filler such as lactose (milk sugar) or sorbitol (an artificial sweetener).

Fentanyl analogs produce effects similar to those of heroin, so heroin addicts looking for a substitute drug sometimes pay top dollar to snort or inject a powder that is mostly milk sugar. For outlaw drugmakers, designer drugs like the fentanyl analogs are almost too good to be true: cheap to make, but expensive on the street.

Amphetamines

Amphetamines are a group of synthetic analogs derived from a natural **stimulant** called ephedrine, which comes from the ephedra plant. Ephedrine is useful for the treatment of asthma, but it also appears in more dangerous preparations such as diet pills and so-called herbal Ecstasy.

Users who inject drugs run a great risk of contracting HIV, the virus that causes AIDS, from contaminated needles. They also can become infected or even die from a drug that has been "cut" with cheap fillers. To keep their own costs low, unscrupulous dealers use fillers like sugar, flour, and rat poison.

Scientists first made amphetamine from ephedrine in 1932. During the 1940s, methamphetamine and dextroamphetamine followed. Scientists noticed that amphetamine and its analogs made people more alert and energetic. Amphetamine drugs also reduced users' appetites. They were the active ingredients in many diet and cold pills until the 1970s.

Before most people became aware of the addictive nature of amphetamines, they had become widely available. Soldiers fighting in World War II used them as energy-boosting "pep pills." The feeling of euphoria (extreme well-being) that comes with an amphetamine rush is deceptive, though. Prolonged use of amphetamine or its analogs can result in **psychosis,** the loss of touch with reality. People who suddenly stop taking amphetamines can suffer a period of extreme exhaustion and depression called "crashing."

Ecstasy

Ecstasy is the most widely used designer drug. It is actually a "child" of methamphetamine. The other parent drug of Ecstasy is MDA (3,4-methylenedioxyamphetamine), a synthetic hallucinogen that became available in the 1960s as an alternative to LSD. Known as the "love drug" because it enhances warm feelings toward others, MDA became illegal after the FDA placed it on Schedule I in 1970. To stay one step ahead of the law, illegal drug manufacturers combined MDA with methamphetamine to create MDMA (3,4-methylenedioxymethamphetamine), or Ecstasy, also known as "Stacy," "X," "lover's speed," or "clarity."

Because it is an analog of MDA and methamphetamine, Ecstasy is considered a hallucinogenic amphetamine—it combines the effects of both drugs. Ecstasy users report that its hallucinogenic properties cause them to perceive sights, smells, sensations, and sounds more vividly. An Ecstasy high makes users more talkative and seems to break down emotional barriers.

Phencyclidine (PCP) and Its Analogs

Ecstasy users buy the drug for its **main effect** (the chief change the drug makes to bodily functions), which is an energizing rush of loving feelings. People who buy PCP want this drug for its chief **side effect** (a secondary, and usually unwanted, effect from a drug), which is powerful hallucinations. PCP was originally created during the 1950s for use as a surgical **anesthetic** (a substance that causes a loss of feeling or consciousness and therefore helps to relieve pain). Its main effect was to numb pain without slowing down a patient's heartbeat or breathing. While it did just that for people in surgery, PCP also had alarming side effects. Patients given PCP sometimes experienced horrifying hallucinations. Male patients recovering from PCP anesthetic often became physically aggressive.

Although taken off the market, PCP was sold on the street by illegal drug dealers. Given the name PCP, short for "peace pill," it developed a following among people who found the drug's wild, scary side effects exciting. But PCP distorts a user's sense of reality, leads to violent or suicidal behavior, and can even leave the user in a coma.

Fentanyl Analogs

Fentanyl came onto the legal drug market in 1968 as a pain reliever for use during major surgery. It falls into the category of **opioid** drugs. Opioids are similar to and have many of the same effects on the body as opium, a naturally occurring painkiller derived from the poppy

Doctors stopped using phencyclidine, PCP, as a painkiller during surgery when it produced hallucinations and violent behavior in patients. But it soon turned up on the street in the form of a powder called "angel dust." Dealers often lace marijuana with this dangerous drug, or they sell it as mescaline, a hallucinogen made from a cactus called mescal.

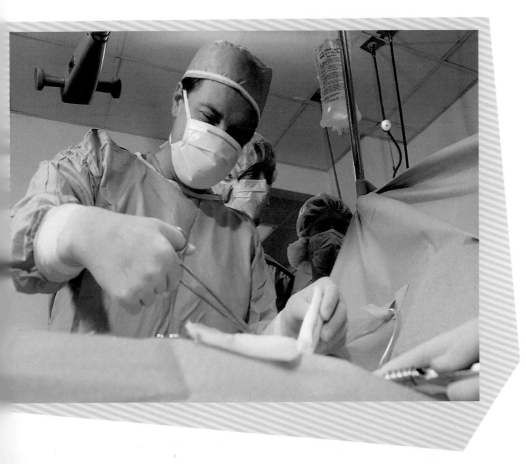

plant called *Papaver somniferum*. The difference is that opioids are not made from opium but are synthetic. Drugs that are derived naturally from opium are called **opiates.** Fentanyl is about 40 times stronger than morphine, a powerful opiate.

Illegal drug manufacturers started making fentanyl analogs in the 1980s that were 80 to 1,000 times stronger than heroin. Heroin, another opiate, is itself almost three times as strong as morphine. Drugmakers also created fentanyl analogs that extended the length of the high.

Because fentanyl and its analogs act like opiates in the body, **cross-tolerance** is possible. That is, a heroin addict can temporarily satisfy his or her physical craving for more heroin with either morphine or fentanyl. A fentanyl addict can do the same with morphine or heroin. Drugmakers sometimes market fentanyl analogs as "synthetic heroin" to attract heroin addicts who can't find their drug of choice. Fentanyl analogs have street names like "China white," "Tango and Cash," and "goodfella."

The fentanyl analogs are so strong that even a very tiny amount can be deadly. Because of this, it is hard to trace fatal doses of fentanyl in drug abusers' bodies. The National Institute on Drug Abuse places the number of confirmed fentanyl overdose deaths in the United States at more than 150 each year. Fentanyl overdoses kill so swiftly that some drug abusers have died before they could even remove the telltale needles from their arms. Fentanyl analogs kill by slowing down a user's breathing until it stops completely. The drugs may also make the chest muscles contract so tightly that the lungs cannot expand to take in air.

Meperidine Analogs

Meperidine is well known by its trade name, Demerol, as a pain reliever used in hospitals. Although it is useful when used properly, it is also highly addictive. Meperidine and its analogs produce feelings of euphoria soon after they enter the body. Like fentanyl, meperidine is an opioid, so cross-tolerance with opiates is possible.

MPPP is the most commonly synthesized meperidine analog. In addition to the usual health risks involved when taking drugs, MPPP use carries an extra peril. If the person concocting the drug makes a mistake, he or she can accidentally produce an extremely dangerous compound called MPTP. When users unknowingly inject MPTP they suffer a terrible burning sensation, and may become immobile and be unable to talk. That is exactly what happened in 1982 to several heroin addicts in the San Francisco area when they injected MPTP into their bodies. We will discuss this tragedy in depth in chapter 3.

Any illegal designer drug can be deadly. In the case of designer meperidine, however, one bad batch can also leave a young person trapped inside an immobile body.

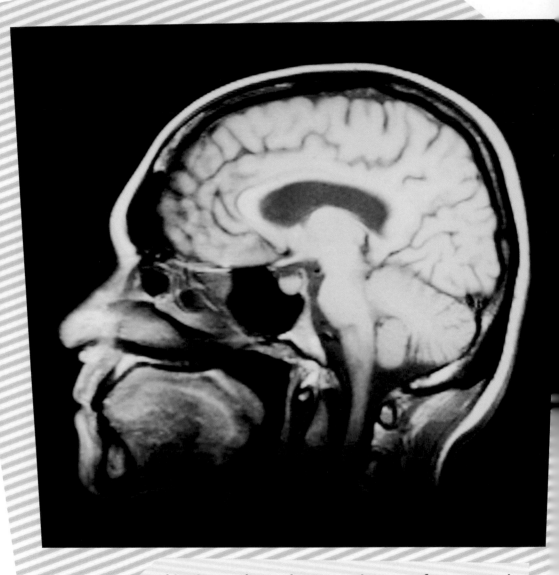

This picture shows the two main parts of your central nervous system—the brain and the spinal cord. The brain is the control center of your body. It sends out and receives messages from your body through the spinal cord. All drugs, including designer drugs, affect how your brain and spinal cord work.

SYNTHETIC DRUGS, GENUINE DANGERS

What is the definition of a drug? A drug is any substance people take orally (by mouth), inhale, smoke, or inject into their veins to alter the way their bodies function. Some drugs are also applied directly onto the skin, but none of the designer drugs fits this description. Designer drugs are not a single type of drug. The only thing all of them have in common is that they are analogs.

Designer drugs affect the **central nervous system,** or CNS, whose main parts are the brain and the spinal cord. Addictive drugs affect the central nervous system's **neurotransmitters** by binding to the **receptor sites** in the brain where neurotransmitters normally bind. Neurotransmitters are chemicals released by nerve cells that carry messages between the cells. They do all this by relaying impulses that originate in the brain from one nerve cell, or **neuron**, to the next. Between nerve endings are tiny gaps called **synapses**. Neurotransmitters carry commands from one synapse to the next and from your brain to other parts of your body. The next time you throw a ball or walk down a flight of stairs, imagine these chemical messengers hard at work, speeding your brain's instructions from synapse to synapse to get your arms and legs moving!

Ecstasy and other designer drugs work by tricking the CNS into thinking that these drugs are your body's own neurotransmitters. Only certain neurotransmitters facilitate movement. Others are "custom-made" to regulate your breathing or elevate your mood. Each type of neurotransmitter goes only to its specific receptor sites in the synapses. For example, some pain receptors get messages exclusively from neurotransmitters called **endorphins,** brain chemicals responsible for pain relief.

Scientists liken receptors and neurotransmitters to locks and keys. Neurotransmitters are "keys" made to unlock only specific receptors. Once unlocked, the receptors send the neurotransmitters' messages throughout your CNS. The effects of different designer drugs depend upon which neurotransmitters they mimic. For example, amphetamines speed up your bodily functions. Fentanyl and meperidine analogs are **depressants** that slow down a user's pulse and breathing. Ecstasy and PCP are **psychoactive** drugs—substances that alter the way your mind works.

Amphetamines

Amphetamines first became available over the counter in 1932 in the form of Benzedrine, a cure for stuffy noses. People in search of clear nasal passages got a lot more than they bargained for when they took it. The amphetamine elevated their mood, increased their alertness, and suppressed their appetites. Although amphetamines are no longer marketed as decongestants, some doctors still occasionally prescribe them for weight loss.

Another use of amphetamines is to help manage the behavior of hyperactive children. This drug that causes a surge of energy in adults seems to help hyperactive children concentrate on one task at a time. The most well known stimulant for treating hyperactive children is a drug called methylphenidate, or Ritalin.

Amphetamines work by imitating the neurotransmitters **norepinephrine** and **serotonin**. Norepinephrine is associated with alertness, positive feelings, and increased energy. Serotonin helps you maintain a good mood and regular sleep cycles. The amphetamine drugs create feelings of euphoria because they "unlock" the brain's receptors for norepinephrine and serotonin. They push existing reserves of natural neurotransmitters out of the receptors and into the CNS, flooding it with these energy-boosting, feel-good chemicals.

The immediate effects of ingesting, injecting, smoking, or snorting amphetamines become apparent quickly. Reactions include euphoria, decreased sensitivity to pain, physical excitement and energy, increased heart rate and blood pressure, and elevated body temperature. A high from methamphetamine, a frequently abused designer drug, can last as long as 12 hours. During this time, a user's brain literally can't calm down.

Methamphetamine in particular also damages the brain's receptors for **dopamine,** a neurotransmitter that enables you to move. Researchers are concerned that as methamphetamine users age, they may develop paralysis if the nerve cells can't repair themselves.

Even one-time amphetamine use can lead to psychosis. A single dose can also cause tremors, rapid and irregular heartbeat, high blood pressure, and fever. People who die from amphetamine overdoses often do so from convulsions as a result of skyrocketing blood pressure.

Even if you survive the ill effects of amphetamine use, you risk the pain of addiction. Your body quickly develops a **tolerance** to amphetamines. Pretty soon, you'll need a dosage high enough to kill a first-time user in order to get the same level of high you once felt. If no amphetamine is available, you'll experience intense physical cravings, difficulty feeling pleasure, and extreme fatigue.

The symptoms that result when a user stops taking an addictive drug are called **withdrawal.** Depression and low energy set in, a result of depleted levels of serotonin and norepinephrine in the brain. Some research suggests that long-term amphetamine use causes brain damage that permanently lowers serotonin and norepinephrine production.

Despite these risks, amphetamines are a widely abused designer drug group. In recent years, a form of amphetamine called methamphetamine ("meth") has hit the streets. Designer drugmakers have taken methamphetamine powder and crystallized it into small, clear rocks. Users smoke this "ice" or "crystal" with glass pipes. Ice is popular because it is highly concentrated

Amphetamines help manage the behavior of hyperactive children. This drug, which causes a surge of energy in adults, seems to help hyperactive children concentrate on one task at a time.

Jessica Laverne Smith was only 14 when she died from an overdose of methamphetamine in 1998. A relative reported that Jessica felt out of control of her life. Many young people who feel they cannot cope with the pressures of daily life may turn to "meth" in an effort to escape from reality. But drug abuse always creates even greater problems.

and fast-acting. Users can get a quick, strong high without using needles. Ice is also extremely addictive.

Fentanyl Analogs

Most fentanyl analog users buy these drugs as substitutes to satisfy their cravings for heroin. Or heroin addicts may unknowingly purchase fentanyls marketed as heroin by drug dealers.

As an opioid drug, fentanyl is highly addictive. Legitimate chemists have tried to "design" this trait out of fentanyl and the other opioids but have had no success. Despite its potential for abuse, fentanyl is a valuable medical tool because of its pain-relieving qualities. But as a designer drug, it can be deadly. One fentanyl analog, China white, first showed up in Orange County, California, in 1979. By 1985, China white and other fentanyl analogs had killed at least 100 people. These deadly designer drugs also caused multiple deaths in Pennsylvania and New York State during the early 1990s.

Fentanyl analogs trick the body into thinking that they are endorphins. If you've ever accidentally dropped something heavy on your foot, your endorphins have probably come to your rescue. The initial injury hurts a lot, but the pain becomes manageable fairly quickly. This relief occurs because soothing endorphins have sped through your CNS to the spot that hurts. Without endorphins, the normal functioning of our bones, joints, and organ systems might be too painful to bear.

When designer fentanyl or another opioid drug enters the brain, it binds to endorphin receptor sites to create a feeling of extreme well-being and tranquillity. When fentanyl replaces endorphins at receptor sites, the brain becomes accustomed to having the drug in order to function normally. This is how a user may become addicted.

A person addicted to fentanyl analogs is literally replacing a natural neurotransmitter with an artificial one. Since the body can't make fentanyls, withdrawal symptoms occur whenever the addict can't refill the receptors with it or another related drug. Withdrawal from fentanyl analogs is physically painful because the brain has adapted to require regular doses of the drug.

PCP and Its Analogs

Phencyclidine (PCP) is a synthetic hallucinogen. It causes users to see, feel, and hear things that aren't really there, including terrifying hallucinations. Usually taken in pill form or snorted in powder form, called "angel dust," PCP also causes decreased touch sensitivity and extreme excitement that can lead to violence or suicidal behavior. People on PCP are prone to hurting themselves as well as others.

Research has not yielded very many clues about how PCP works in the central nervous system. It is unclear which receptors in the brain are sensitive to PCP. Since the early 1990s, authorities have identified a few PCP analogs for sale on the street.

Ecstasy

Ecstasy (MDMA) does not fit neatly into any one category in terms of its effects on the body, because it is both a mild hallucinogen and a stimulant. Since it became widely available in the 1980s, Ecstasy has also become the most popular designer drug among young

Fentanyl analogs act within seconds, producing an intense rush of euphoria along with decreased pain perception. But they are potentially deadly. A user's blood pressure, breathing, and pulse rate can plummet, and chest muscles may spasm, leaving the user unable to breathe.

people. Although many users mistakenly consider Ecstasy a "safe" drug, it is important to examine its potentially dangerous effects.

Ecstasy is a powder usually pressed into pills or put into capsules. People start to feel its effects about half

Did You Know?

On rare occasions, Ecstasy actually kills people. Most Ecstasy-related deaths are the result of heat stroke. The drug causes hyperthermia, a sharply elevated body temperature that can quickly reach more than 105 degrees. A fever this high is dangerous in itself, but it also causes dehydration. The combination of severe dehydration and elevated temperature can permanently damage the liver and kidneys. Left untreated, heat stroke can lead to convulsions and death.

an hour after ingesting it. Most report an initial high lasting about one hour. During this time, users feel energetic, confident, warm, and loving as physical boundaries seem to melt away. Some people feel like they're floating on air or that their arms and legs are weightless. After the initial rush wears off, users feel mellow and free of anger. This stage usually lasts about three to four hours. It is followed by a "chill-out" period lasting about eight hours.

Ecstasy acts like the neurotransmitter serotonin, pushing natural serotonin out into the CNS while the drug binds to serotonin receptor sites. This explains the initial rush of euphoria one feels after taking the drug.

The Downside of Ecstasy

So far, you might think that an Ecstasy trip doesn't sound too bad. Some users experience such uncomfortable physical symptoms, however, that no high is worth the suffering. Ecstasy can cause nausea and vomiting.

Most users experience muscle tension, rapid eye-blinking, and jaw clenching. Many also feel light-headed and perspire excessively.

Ecstasy causes an irregular heartbeat and raises body temperature. There have been reported cases of psychosis resulting from taking Ecstasy. A small number of users experience "flashbacks" that haunt them even after the drug wears off. Others become paranoid or suffer terrifying panic attacks. This is probably because of Ecstasy's amphetamine-like properties.

Ecstasy users will feel chills and have sore muscles as the drug's effects wear off. Depression may set in because the brain is momentarily low on serotonin. Ecstasy does not seem to cause physical dependence, but some people are convinced they need it simply because life without Ecstasy seems dull and colorless by comparison. This is called psychological dependence.

Using Ecstasy repeatedly causes the user to develop a tolerance to the drug. There is new evidence that a user's bleak mood may be the result of actual brain damage. A study in the 1980s conducted on 14 people in London who had used Ecstasy showed that their brains contained fewer serotonin receptors than the brains of people who had never used the drug. Because Ecstasy killed brain cells in laboratory animals, the study confirmed what scientists had assumed: Ecstasy is a **neurotoxin** for human beings. Neurotoxins are substances that are poisonous to the CNS.

Ecstasy with Other Drugs

Ecstasy becomes even more dangerous when used in combination with other drugs. Young people who frequent clubs sometimes take it together with the powerful hallucinogen LSD, a practice known as "candy flipping." The resulting hallucinations are much more intense—

Prolonged use of Ecstasy often leads to deep depression. Users suffer from great sadness and dejection, often crying uncontrollably. They may feel overcome by a sense of hopelessness, which can sometimes lead to suicidal tendencies.

and potentially frightening—than those experienced on Ecstasy alone. Candy flipping puts young people in increased danger of experiencing psychoses and flashbacks after the drugs have worn off.

In addition, some people wash down Ecstasy tablets with alcohol. Both alcohol and Ecstasy dehydrate the user's body. In combination, these two drugs can swiftly sicken or even kill the unsuspecting user.

Herbal and Liquid Ecstasy

Herbal Ecstasy is legal under current federal drug laws. People buy it thinking they are safe because it is legal. Although herbal Ecstasy has no chemical relation to the drug Ecstasy, this is a dangerous mistake. Herbal Ecstasy is available over the counter, and young people in search of what they think is a safe, natural rush may take as many as four pills at a time. Brand names include Cloud 9, Ultimate Xphoria, and Rave Energy.

Makers of herbal Ecstasy promise raised consciousness and "inner visions." What most users actually get is tingly skin, nervousness, and a tremor because the active ingredient in herbal Ecstasy is ephedra, a stimulant. Herbal Ecstasy also contains caffeine. Federal authorities have received more than 800 reports of adverse reactions to herbal Ecstasy. Symptoms include high blood pressure, seizures, strokes, and heart attacks. Some users have even died.

Another drug that has no chemical relationship to Ecstasy is GHB (gamma hydroxybutyrate). It goes by the street names "Liquid Ecstasy," "Liquid X," and

Herbal Ecstasy is openly displayed in a "head" shop, a store that sells drug devices such as pipes. Because herbal Ecstasy is classified by the FDA as a supplement, it is not regulated the way drugs are. Despite warnings by the government of herbal Ecstasy's potentially dangerous side effects, it is currently legal to buy and sell this substance.

"Grievous Bodily Harm." In addition to the clear, salty-tasting liquid form, sold in vials, GHB also comes in capsules containing a powder. In fact, some people who think they're buying Ecstasy are actually purchasing GHB capsules.

The similarities end there, however. Unlike Ecstasy, GHB depresses the central nervous system after an initial euphoric rush. Since 1990 the FDA has considered GHB a Schedule II drug that can be used only under medical supervision. Some drug experts consider GHB the scourge of the future among designer drugs. Within 15 minutes of sipping it or mixing it into a drink, GHB users experience euphoria and deep relaxation.

But GHB can also cause dangerously high temperature, dizziness, nausea, shortness of breath, rigid muscles, seizures, coma, and death. Doctors say that users may appear to be fine, then suddenly collapse. The Drug Enforcement Agency (DEA) counted 17 GHB-related deaths nationwide from March 1995 to February 1997. Since GHB is a relative newcomer to the designer drug scene, those numbers are likely to climb.

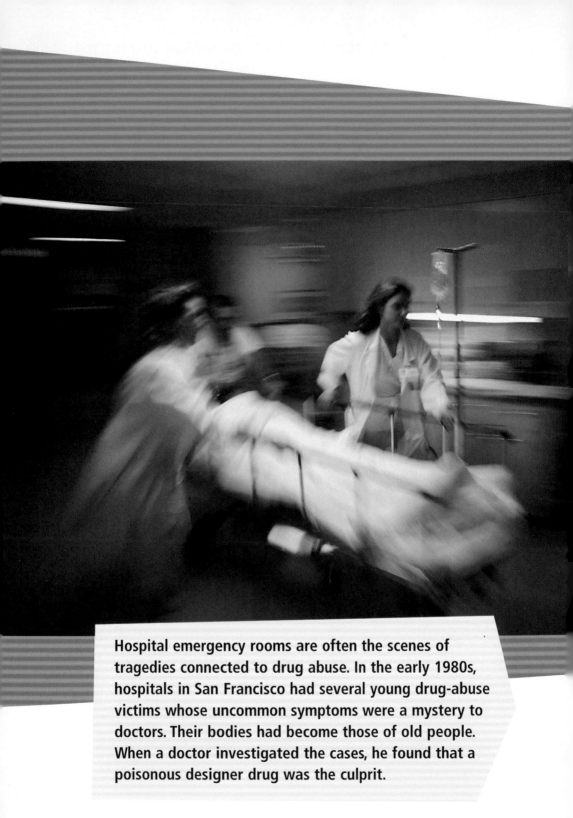

Hospital emergency rooms are often the scenes of tragedies connected to drug abuse. In the early 1980s, hospitals in San Francisco had several young drug-abuse victims whose uncommon symptoms were a mystery to doctors. Their bodies had become those of old people. When a doctor investigated the cases, he found that a poisonous designer drug was the culprit.

DESIGNER POISON

On July 16, 1982, Dr. William Langston, a neurologist at California's Santa Clara Valley Medical Center, got his first glimpse of a patient who would change the course of his career. A 42-year-old heroin addict named George Carillo lay in a hospital bed, unable to move or speak. Langston described him this way: "His mouth was slightly open and drooled continuously. His arms were bent at his side with the elbows outward, as if frozen midway through a motion. He made no sound."

As July wore on, five similar cases came to Langston's attention. One of them was George Carillo's girlfriend: she had shared what she believed to be heroin with George before they both became ill. All six patients were from the San Francisco Bay area. All of them also had in common their abuse of heroin. Every one of them had gotten sick within hours or days of injecting "synthetic heroin." Their doctors were baffled. What followed was a medical detective story. It is a mystery in which the designer drug industry is the villain.

First, Langston and the other doctors caring for the "frozen" addicts determined that they suffered from Parkinson's disease, or Parkinsonism. It is a progressive, nervous-system disease that almost never strikes people under the age of 50. These six patients, however, ranged in age from just 21 to 42 years. Still more confusing, Langston's patients all showed symptoms of very advanced Parkinson's disease—symptoms that usually take years to develop. Langston suspected that a bad batch of heroin had poisoned the six addicts, but how?

Dr. Langston knew that he had to do two things: track down samples of the drug that had paralyzed the addicts and warn other drug users about the dangerous heroin for sale on the street. He called a press conference that alerted some 20 million

What Causes Parkinson's Disease?

Parkinson's disease is a degenerative brain condition in which a small section of the brain called the substantia nigra is destroyed. The substantia nigra produces dopamine, a neurotransmitter that controls voluntary movement. Without dopamine, the urge to move your legs does not reach the nerves and muscles that actually get the job done. In Parkinson's disease the substantia nigra becomes damaged and cannot produce enough dopamine. Victims suffer body trembling and rigid muscles. Parkinson's disease advances with age until, in later stages, its victims are unable to move, speak, or feed themselves.

Parkinson's disease can strike anyone when the brain gradually stops producing enough of the neurotransmitter dopamine. Although the disease is generally a condition of advancing age, the illegal drug MPTP can cause Parkinsonism in young people. A new, legal drug called Sinemet, a kind of artificial dopamine, can help these victims. However, the remedy lasts only from three to five years, and then the condition may recur.

local TV viewers. After police found drug samples in the victims' homes, an analytic chemist discovered that the powder they had injected was not heroin at all, but a tainted designer drug.

A toxicologist (a scientist who deals with poisons and their effects) named Halle Weingarten identified the drug as a meperidine analog, one of the designer drugs favored by heroin addicts when their drug of choice is not available.

The development of designer drugs by pharmaceutical companies is strictly controlled by the government. Drugs are tested and retested in laboratories to ensure their quality and safety. After testing, people may take the drugs only under careful clinical monitoring. Illegal drugs are not tested. They may cause totally unexpected results, contain poisonous substances, or not even be what drug dealers claim them to be.

It was Halle Weingarten's sharp memory that helped identify the dangerous analog as MPTP. She remembered an article in an old medical journal about a young man who had developed Parkinson's disease after using meperidine analogs. The young man was a college student named Barry Kidston, who was addicted to Demerol (the trade name for meperidine). In the summer of 1976, Kidston tried to make a nonaddictive version of Demerol. He used his chemistry set to make the meperidine analog MPPP. That November, Kidston "froze up," unable to move or speak. His doctors "unfroze" him with L-dopa, a drug used to treat Parkinson's patients.

Although his condition was being monitored at the National Institutes of Health (NIH) in Bethesda, Maryland, Barry Kidston could not stop abusing drugs. He died in 1978 from an overdose of cocaine. Making and using designer meperidine had cost him his health and, eventually, his life.

A chemist named Sanford Markey used Barry's notes to replicate the young man's attempts to make MPPP. He also examined Barry's chemistry set for traces of residue from batches of designer meperidine. The substance Sanford Markey found was MPTP. Dr. Langston had his culprit. He was now certain that the six heroin addicts he was studying had Parkinson's disease caused by MPTP. When he began treating them with L-dopa, they responded dramatically, quickly regaining the ability to walk and talk.

In the course of his investigation, Dr. Langston learned just how dangerous MPTP was. In 1983, he received a letter from a legitimate chemist who had been exposed to MPTP during the 1960s and 1970s and had been diagnosed with Parkinson's disease at the age of 39. The chemist became sick after only minimal contact with MPTP. He had either accidentally inhaled its vapors or had simply touched the compound without wearing gloves. Dr. Langston also learned of two drug addicts in Vancouver, Canada, who had unknowingly snorted a meperidine analog tainted with MPTP. By 1985, both had developed severe Parkinsonism—and one had died.

That year, the Centers for Disease Control in Atlanta, Georgia, identified 147 people who had used the tainted designer meperidine in 1982. While none of them showed definite symptoms of Parkinson's disease at the time, their chances of good health in the future were questionable.

The MPTP tragedy in northern California eventually brought Dr. Langston face-to-face with the man authorities blamed for the bad batch of synthetic heroin that had caused so much suffering. On March 22, 1985, police escorted Vincent Mason, a former lawyer who was now serving time in a Texas jail for manufacturing PCP, into Langston's California office. Mason had operated a designer drug lab in northern California during 1981 and 1982. Police suspected him of making the tainted meperidine analog that had crippled Langston's six patients. Nearly three years after this disaster, Vincent Mason wanted Dr. Langston to give him a medical examination. The designer drug manufacturer now feared that he, too, had Parkinson's disease. Dr. Langston checked Mason and found no signs of Parkinsonism.

Although Mason had probably poisoned Langston's patients, they themselves were also responsible for what had happened to them. They had injected themselves with the tainted designer drugs. But even commercial chemists who did nothing more than handle MPTP in the course of their work could get Parkinson's disease.

Although L-dopa unfroze Dr. Langston's patients, he knew that it was not a cure-all. L-dopa loses its effectiveness over time, requiring Parkinson's patients to take increasingly frequent dosages. The drug also produces tolerance, so that people need to take more and more L-dopa to remain mobile.

In 1982, six young people suddenly found themselves trapped in old, sickly bodies because of a poorly made designer drug. MPTP is a "designer mistake," a dangerous by-product that forms when MPPP is improperly made. In the crude laboratories of amateur chemists, this kind of contamination is a very real possibility with every new batch of drugs.

Dr. Langston's work with the "frozen addicts" shed light on the causes of Parkinson's disease and eventually led to a new surgical treatment. But these gains were made at a terrible cost. None of the patients who accidentally poisoned themselves with MPTP would ever completely regain his or her health. In fact, one of the six died and the rest required specialized care for the remainder of their lives.

Designer drugs—often impure, and always unpredictable—can exact a stiff price for a quick high. The 1982 tragedy in northern California could repeat itself anytime or anywhere. A similar disaster could happen with any other designer drug, too. With designer drugs, you can never be sure of exactly what it is you are putting into your body.

Young people want to have fun and often turn to drugs to enhance their pleasure with friends at clubs and parties. Expectations of having a good time and getting positive feelings can influence their choice of drug. In the 1980s, Ecstasy was the drug of choice when young people began gathering at all-night dance parties called "raves." Although banned in 1985 because of its harmful side effects, Ecstasy is still widely used illegally.

FROM THERAPY TO THE RAVE SCENE: ECSTASY IN SOCIETY

S et and setting are very important in determining how someone will react to a given drug. A person's expectations and surroundings also influence his or her decision to use drugs in the first place. Young people often experiment with drugs when they are with friends and are anticipating positive effects from a drug. This is true of any drug but especially of Ecstasy. Mental-health workers have given it to their patients, and teens and young adults wanting a good time have tried Ecstasy to see if it could meet their expectations.

In 1965 an American biochemist named Alexander Shulgin developed Ecstasy. Although he worked for Dow Chemical making products like insect repellent, Shulgin was very curious about mind-altering drugs. In 1977, he gave some Ecstasy to a psychotherapist friend for use with his clients.

Before long, glowing reports emerged about the usefulness of Ecstasy in psychiatric settings. The years from 1977 to 1985 have been called the "golden age" of Ecstasy. Some therapists swore by Ecstasy as a way to make their clients less defensive and more able to face their problems honestly. In fact, therapists gave Ecstasy the nickname "Adam" because they said it made clients who took it as open and worry-free as the biblical Adam when he lived in the Garden of Eden.

Then, in 1985, the U.S. Drug Enforcement Agency banned the manufacture, possession, and use of Ecstasy by giving it Schedule I status. The government decided to criminalize Ecstasy because people were using it at nightclubs and bars, where they could sometimes buy it openly. Scientists were also beginning to question whether Ecstasy was a neurotoxin.

In 1985 there was no proof that Ecstasy was dangerous. Some therapists opposed the ban, reporting that the drug had been successful in treating many patients who usually could not deal with reality.

Set and setting were probably important factors in the success of some therapies involving Ecstasy. Clients probably hoped and expected to get better by using this new drug. They were also taking it in a safe, protected place with a therapist to monitor their safety.

At the same time that therapists were discontinuing the use of Ecstasy, the drug was becoming increasingly popular among college students and other young adults. Use of the drug started out in California, Florida, and Texas nightclubs, but soon spread around the country. Users liked the way it increased their self-confidence and energy at crowded parties and bars. Many of Ecstasy's new American fans thought they had found the ultimate party drug: a safe, invigorating mood brightener. They were mentally "set" for fun when they took Ecstasy. Then, in 1991, the scene changed when "rave" parties began in San Francisco. Raves are dance parties held in secret locations like vacant warehouses or open fields. Hundreds, or even

Therapists usually treat their clients in a one-on-one setting. They may use certain drugs to help relieve a client's anxiety or stress, but Ecstasy is no longer one of them. The drug may have helped some clients face difficult problems, but its potential to damage the central nervous system caused the government to ban its use for both medical and recreational purposes.

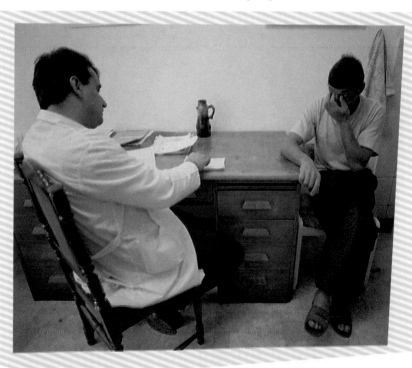

thousands, of young people attend by purchasing tickets with only a phone number on them. They then call for directions on the night of the rave so that authorities won't learn of the location and shut the party down beforehand. Some raves advertise by word-of-mouth alone. Ecstasy was the drug of choice at raves, and it would shape a whole new setting and drug culture in the United States.

Most young people do not use drugs. Still, a 1998 nationwide study revealed that 45 percent of twelfth graders had used illegal drugs at least once. Thirty percent said they had used drugs before high school. Many young people often think that they are taking drugs only for "recreational" use and can quit anytime. In most cases, however, therapy and counseling are necessary to overcome drug addiction.

The sole purpose of a rave is to dance all night. Young people crowd into a warehouse or onto a field and move to techno music with its electronic sound and hypnotic beat. Raves often feature lasers and flashing lights along with the music. Techno DJs usually play song after song without stopping to banter with the ravers.

This is because most ravers want to lose themselves in the sights and sounds around them, and they do it with Ecstasy. It is not unusual to see dancers hugging and gently running their hands over each other at raves. This is an effect of Ecstasy, the "hug drug." Ravers who use Ecstasy often report that the drug, the music and lights, and the dancing combine to put them in a blissful trance.

Ecstasy has become the most popular designer drug among young people at raves. But they also use other drugs such as LSD, amphetamines, GHB, and a strong sedative called rohypnol. Many people refer to Ecstasy as one of the "club drugs."

Use of Ecstasy is not limited to young adults or ravers. Even a few junior high schoolers experiment with it as a way to mellow out at home. Six percent of twelfth graders, more than 5.5 percent of tenth graders, and more than 3 percent of eighth graders surveyed in 1996 had used Ecstasy at least once in their lives. Another survey showed that overall drug use among 11- to 14-year-olds is rising faster than that of any other group. Most American kids do not use Ecstasy, or any other designer drugs. The small group that does, however, is getting younger and younger.

In the Canadian province of Ontario, the percentage of kids who admit to using Ecstasy is also small. A survey taken every two years shows that in 1994 the total rate of students in grades 7, 9, 11, and 13 who used Ecstasy was not quite 2 percent. But that small figure had more than doubled from the 1993 rate of 0.6 percent. Boys were more than twice as likely to use Ecstasy as girls, and more eleventh and thirteenth graders used it than did seventh and ninth graders. Whether you're growing up in the United States or Canada, Ecstasy—like most drugs—appears to become more readily available as you get older.

Whatever their age, Ecstasy users risk ruining their health with every dose. They have no way of knowing if that tablet they've blown $30 on is really Ecstasy until they ingest it. If it is the "real thing," Ecstasy can cause kidney failure, heatstroke, death, and brain damage.

If you go to rave parties simply because you enjoy dancing, staying drug-free means that you will know when to stop before you overheat or injure yourself. You will also be alert enough to protect yourself or your friends from trouble in a noisy, crowded environment. Some under-21 clubs now offer special alcohol-free rave nights, where you can have the rave experience in a safe, legal place.

Social Risks

Whether or not you're an avid raver, the risks of Ecstasy use are great. Some risks are purely physical; others hazards are emotional. Since Ecstasy can remove your inhibitions, you may say or do something harmful or hurtful to yourself or a friend while under its influence.

Other risks have both physical and emotional components. An Ecstasy high may make you less choosy about your "friends." You may mistake drug-induced feelings of warmth and intimacy for love. The hug drug may lead young people to take sexual risks that can lead to disease or unwanted pregnancy. You may end up feeling only sadness and confusion if you act on the emotions that Ecstasy can stir up.

While Ecstasy is dangerous and illegal in any setting, it is also true that environment is often specifically tailored for Ecstasy use. If you experiment with Ecstasy at a crowded rave party, you are in a setting that is custom-made for escaping the worries and responsibilities of life. This carefree atmosphere, however, masks the real physical dangers of Ecstasy.

Trying to escape from your worries with Ecstasy can lead to regular use. And regular use can make daily living especially hard for adolescents. Repeated Ecstasy use may cause giddy highs followed by crushing lows— a cycle that is really disruptive when you are still trying to figure out who you are and what kind of adult you want to become. Or Ecstasy may simply stop making you feel good while still causing unpleasant side effects.

When you examine all the possibilities, Ecstasy hardly seems to live up to its name.

These students in Greenville, South Carolina, are marching to make others more aware of the dangers of drugs. Does your school have a program that teaches drug awareness? If not, maybe you can help start one.

5

DESIGNING A DRUG-FREE LIFE

No matter how old you are, the desire to fit into your social circle is a powerful force. The often unspoken pressure you feel to share the same tastes, values, and interests as other people so that they will accept you is called peer pressure. It can influence the way you behave, dress, or earn a living. When you feel compelled to do something to avoid being rejected by the people in your social group, you are experiencing peer pressure. Your peers—friends, siblings, and others who are close to your own age—fear being excluded just as much as you do.

Most people associate peer pressure with negative behavior such as teasing or being goaded to do something you don't want to do. Many times, however, you feel pressure to do positive things in order to fit in. If you are a student who strives for good grades, for instance, the achievements of your friends who are

The desire to belong and be part of the crowd is probably strongest during the teen years. This makes young people especially vulnerable to trying alcohol, drugs, and cigarettes. Young people need awareness education and the attention and support of adults to help them resist the temptations of drugs.

good students probably inspire you to keep working hard in school.

When it comes to drugs, however, peer pressure is usually a negative force. In the middle- and high-school years, the urge to fit in and be part of the crowd is tremendous. That means young people are especially vulnerable to trying alcohol, cigarettes, and drugs.

It is not always easy to refuse drugs without losing friends. Pro-drug messages are everywhere. Movies and

TV shows sometimes depict drug users and dealers as glamorous risk-takers who are immune to the consequences of their acts. Characters who are drunk or stoned are occasionally portrayed as funny people who lighten up tense situations. Some popular song lyrics celebrate drug use. Even clothing can become a billboard for drugs.

With all the messages we get telling us that drugs equal an exciting life, it is no wonder that many young people have tried drugs. One survey shows that 59 percent of teens said that they were offered drugs in 1997 and that 28 percent of 9- to 12-year-olds were also offered drugs that same year.

Far fewer kids actually use drugs than are offered them, however. The Parents' Resource Institute for Drug Education (PRIDE) reports that "The fact is [that] the largest teen peer group doesn't use drugs." So in reality, most people your age are smart, creative, and mature enough to say "no" to drugs and "yes" to healthy alternatives.

But staying drug-free is more easily said than done. After all, nobody wants to look unsophisticated in the eyes of his or her friends. Suppose you are invited to a weekend party at the home of one of the most popular kids in school. When you get there, however, you find many of the guests are drunk. A knot forms in your stomach. You know that underage drinking and drug abuse are both illegal. More important, you also understand how dangerous they are. You know that you've walked into an unsafe situation, but you're also worried that your friends will think less of you if you refuse to join the "fun." What can you do? You have four choices:

1. You can give in to the pressure, endangering your health—maybe even your life—in the process.

2. You can suggest other activities. Something as simple as a walk or a movie may distract your friends from drinking or taking drugs.

3. You can leave in a way that will not insult your friends. This is one situation in which it is okay to tell a lie: Your parents want you to start dinner before they get home, for example.

4. You can speak out against what your friends are doing, and tell a trusted adult that you fear for their safety. This option probably requires the most courage, but it is well worth the effort.

Doing the right thing is never easy. But alcohol and drug abuse can make peer pressure a life-and-death matter. If friends shut you out because of your stand, remember that they are probably just as scared of being disliked as you are. If they see you—someone who seems just like them—abusing drugs too, then they can tell themselves that it's not such a bad thing.

Chances are good that some of your peers who do abuse drugs also know how dangerous it is but are afraid to speak up. If you take a stand on not using drugs and cigarettes, you may be pleasantly surprised to find at least one other person who agrees with you. If you present a strong example, other people who were afraid to openly disagree with the crowd may very well take your side, too. And if necessary, you can always find a new group of friends to hang out with.

Anyone who tells you that using drugs makes you more sophisticated or adult is lying. In truth, drugs are a great way to delay growing up. They impede your ability

Support from their peers is important for teenagers who want to avoid drugs. It can be difficult to drop some friends and find new ones. But joining a drug-free crowd is worth the effort. Enjoying dances, parties, and other get-togethers with friends who feel the same way is the way to take a stand against drugs. In the end, it will also be more fun, and certainly less risky, than getting high just to fit in.

Taking drugs does not have to be a part of growing up. These teens are using their minds and talents to express themselves through music. Teenagers can direct their energies to many other activities. Taking part in extracurricular school programs and community activities keeps young people busy and can give them a real sense of accomplishment and control over their lives.

to handle responsibility or to face challenges head-on.

Many people take drugs to avoid the pain of even occasional rejections or to banish boredom. They never learn how to deal with disappointment—or how to have fun—without drugs. It is not uncommon for an adolescent who has been using drugs for a long time to have the social skills of someone much younger. Drug abusers risk being left behind socially at school, at games or parties, and on the job.

Some people abuse drugs because the element of physical risk excites them. When they gamble with their health and safety, they feel courageous and daring. If you want to challenge yourself physically, there are far more constructive ways to do it. Taking up a new sport or embarking on a regular workout routine will test your limits *and* make you better, faster, and stronger.

Your friends may drink, smoke, or take drugs because "There's nothing to do around here." Think again! Most communities have an abundance of activities for young people. There are sports teams or clubs. Schools and communities often have music groups. You can do volunteer work or join a church or synagogue youth group. You can enjoy a part-time job; it gives you a sense of accomplishment and some money. Kids who take on activities like these are probably too busy using their minds and bodies to be sidelined by drug highs and hangovers.

If you say "no" to drugs—and your friends can't— you may have to find new companions. It is not always easy, but forging new friendships with kids who don't do drugs is worth the effort. But what if a good friend has started abusing drugs? How can you help? First, ask yourself some questions about your friend's behavior. Look at the questionnaire on page 67 and think about answers to the questions.

If you suspect that a friend or family member has a substance-abuse problem, you might be afraid to approach him or her. Sometimes it is helpful to talk to a parent, teacher, counselor, or other trusted adult beforehand. There are also numerous telephone hotlines and Internet sites available (see pages 73–75) where you can get tips on how to cope when a friend or loved one abuses drugs. But remember that you cannot control another person's behavior; only the substance abuser can decide to quit. Sometimes, however, just knowing that you care will encourage others to get the help they need.

Provided that your friend or loved one is not behaving in a violent or threatening way, you might try to discuss the problem using these guidelines:

- Be certain that your friend is abusing drugs. Drug abusers tend to deny or minimize their problem.

- Pick a time when you are both calm and in a private setting.

- Don't rush in and accuse. Talk quietly and kindly.

- Offer to help your friend find treatment and even go with him or her.

If it seems that your conversation has no impact, don't despair. Sometimes people do not want to hear the truth about how others see them. Unless your friend threatens you or lashes out at you, leave the door to friendship open. Explain that you can't hang out with him or her as long as drugs are in the picture but that you hope the two of you can resume the activities you used to enjoy together. Your friend will know you care; you'll know you made your best effort.

? Questions To Ask Yourself About Your Friend's Behavior

❏ Does he/she use drugs or alcohol regularly?

❏ Does he/she lie to cover up the amount of alcohol or drugs consumed?

❏ Can he/she have a good time without drugs or alcohol?

❏ Does he/she frequently talk about drinking or doing drugs?

❏ Does he/she spend time alone drinking or doing drugs, or has he/she dropped old friends and activities?

❏ Has his/her attendance or performance at school or work suffered because of drinking or drug use?

❏ Does he/she pressure other people to drink or use drugs?

❏ Has he/she gotten into trouble with the police?

❏ Does he/she engage in risky behavior, such as driving or having sex while under the influence of alcohol or drugs?

While you want to help your friend, be aware that you do not want to become an enabler. An enabler is someone who, through words or actions, makes it easier for another person to continue self-destructive behaviors. If you lend money to a friend knowing that he or she is likely to spend it on drugs, you are enabling that friend to continue abusing drugs. If you tell "white lies" to cover up a friend's drug problem, you are helping him or her continue a dangerous habit. You should refuse to do anything that will make it easy for others to smoke, snort, inject, ingest, or drink without getting caught.

What if you're the one who might be in trouble with drugs? Determine the extent of the problem by answering honestly the questions in the box on page 69.

Treatment can be outpatient or inpatient. As an outpatient client, you attend scheduled therapy sessions and go home between appointments. Inpatient centers are often more intensive. Clients live at the treatment facility for a certain number of days. Therapy can be individual, or groups or families can get help together. Treatment programs and facilities are available to fit every budget.

Nobody needs to fight a drug problem alone. Moreover, a person probably shouldn't, since there is really no such thing as a "former" drug addict. Even after an addict becomes drug-free, he or she will always be especially vulnerable to becoming hooked again. For this reason, a drug addict who remains straight is said to be "in recovery." This means abstaining from one's drug of abuse—as well as any other drug not prescribed by a doctor. A recovering addict's brain is permanently programmed to crave the good feelings that drug abuse once provided.

People who seek and follow appropriate treatment for drug problems have every reason to be optimistic about the future.

Still, the best way to fight drug addiction is to

Questions To Ask Yourself About Your Behavior

❑ Do you think that you need drugs to have fun?

❑ Have drugs affected your schoolwork or job performance?

❑ Do drugs make you feel relaxed after stressful events?

❑ Are you uncertain about whether you will use drugs on any given day?

❑ Do you need increasing amounts of drugs for the same effect that smaller amounts once gave you?

❑ Do you use drugs or drink when you are alone?

❑ Do you make promises not to use drugs only to break them?

If you answer yes to even one of these questions, you may need expert help to get drugs out of your life. Tell a trusted adult that you need to find treatment, or call a toll-free hotline (see pages 73–74).

avoid using drugs in the first place. Growing up is hard enough without riding a roller coaster of highs and hangovers. You'll probably look back on the journey to adulthood as a fun and rewarding time someday. Even though the challenges of growing up sometimes seem overwhelming, your adolescence is much too exciting to waste even one moment on drugs.

GLOSSARY

anesthetic—a substance that causes loss of feeling or consciousness and therefore helps to relieve pain.

analog—a new drug that is almost chemically identical to an existing drug.

central nervous system (CNS)—part of the nervous system consisting of the brain and spinal cord that controls all incoming and outgoing impulses in the body.

cross-tolerance—A condition in which a drug user with a tolerance to one drug develops a tolerance to a drug with similar effects.

depressant—a substance that reduces the rate of your body's functioning.

designer drug—a synthetic drug produced by chemically altering the structure of an original (often illegal) drug, or a drug that has been redesigned to increase appeal.

dopamine—a neurotransmitter in the brain. Dopamine is released by neurons in the limbic system, a part of the brain that controls feelings of pleasure.

drug—any substance taken to alter the way the body functions.

endorphin—a chemical in the brain responsible for pain relief.

hallucinogen—a substance that distorts the user's perception of objects or events or causes the user to perceive objects or visions that are not real.

main effect—the chief change a drug makes to bodily functioning.

marijuana—drug from the leaves of the *Cannabis sativa* plan.

molecule—the smallest chemical unit of a substance containing all the properties of that substance.

neuron—a nerve cell.

neurotoxin—a poison that damages the central nervous system.

neurotransmitter—a chemical that is released by neurons and carries messages between them.

norepinephrine—a neurotransmitter in the brain. Norepinephrine helps to prepare the mind and body for emergencies by widening breathing tubes and making the heart beat faster.

opiate—a drug derived naturally from opium.

opioid—any synthetic drug that is not derived from opium but shares many of opium's chemical properties.

parent drug—a drug from which a designer drug is derived.

psychoactive—describes drugs that affect the mind or behavior.

psychosis—mental state in which people lose touch with reality.

receptor site—a special area of a cell that combines with a chemical substance to alter the cell's function.

serotonin—a neurotransmitter involved in the control of mood, aggression, and sexual behavior.

side effect—a secondary, and usually unwanted, effect from a drug.

stimulant—a drug that increases the rate at which the body functions.

synapse—a tiny gap between nerve endings that neurotransmitters cross.

tolerance—a condition in which a drug user needs increasing amounts of the drug to achieve the same level of intoxication once obtained from using smaller amounts.

withdrawal—a condition resulting from discontinuing use of an addictive drug. Symptoms may include intense physical cravings and extreme fatigue.

BIBLIOGRAPHY

Alvergue, Anne. *Ecstasy: The Danger of False Euphoria.* New York: Rosen Publishing Group, Inc., 1998.

Goldstein, Avram, M.D. *Addiction: From Biology to Drug Policy.* New York: W. H. Freeman and Company, 1994.

Langston, James William, M.D., and Jon Palfreman. *The Case of the Frozen Addicts.* New York: Pantheon Books, 1995.

Littell, Mary Ann. *LSD.* Springfield, NJ: Enslow Pubishers, Inc., 1996.

Longenecker, Gesina L. *How Drugs Work: Drug Abuse and the Human Body.* Emeryville, CA: Ziff-Davis Press, 1994.

Murdico, Suzanne J. *Drug Abuse.* Austin, TX: Steck-Vaughn Company, 1998.

Myers, Arthur. *Drugs and Peer Pressure.* New York: The Rosen Publishing Group, Inc., 1995.

Partnership for a Drug-Free America. "The Boomer-Rang: Baby Boomers Seriously Underestimate Presence of Drugs in Their Children's Lives." Partnership for a Drug-Free America, April 13, 1997.

Robbins, Paul. *Designer Drugs.* Springfield, NJ: Enslow Publishers, Inc., 1995.

Ross, Emma. "Users of the Drug Ecstasy at Risk of Brain Damage, Researchers Say." *The Philadelphia Inquirer,* October 30, 1998.

Saunders, Nicholas. *E for Ecstasy.* London: Nicholas Saunders, 1993.

Wekesser, Carol, ed. *Chemical Dependency: Opposing Viewpoints.* San Diego: Greenhaven Press, Inc., 1997.

White House Office of National Drug Control Policy. "Juveniles and Drugs." Washington, DC: White House Office of National Drug Control Policy, 1997.

Winsor, Morgan, and Rick Jervis. "New Designer Drug Can Leave Partiers Dazed—or Dead." *Miami Herald,* September 13, 1997.

Yaslow, Mark. *Drugs in the Body.* New York: Franklin Watts, Inc., 1992.

FIND OUT MORE ABOUT DESIGNER DRUGS AND DRUG ABUSE

The following list includes agencies, organizations, and websites that provide information about designer and other drugs. You can also find out where to go for help with a drug problem. Many national organizations have local chapters listed in your phone directory. Look under "Drug Abuse and Addiction" to find resources in your area.

Agencies and Organizations in the United States

American Council for Drug Education
167 West 74th Street
New York, NY 10023
800-488-DRUG (3784)

Center for Substance Abuse Treatment
Information and Treatment Referral Hotline
11426-28 Rockville Pike, Suite 410
Rockville, MD 20852
800-622-HELP (4357)

Hazelden Foundation
P.O. Box 11, CO3
Center City, MN 55012-0011
800-257-7810
http://www.hazelden.org

National Clearinghouse for Alcohol and Drug Information
P. O. Box 2345
Rockville, MD 20847-2345
800-729-6686
http://www.health.org

Narcotics Anonymous
P.O. Box 9999
Van Nuys, CA 91409
818-773-9999

Parents' Resource Institute for Drug Education (PRIDE)
3610 DeKalb Technology Parkway
Suite 105
Atlanta, GA 30340
770-458-9900
http://www.prideusa.org

Addictions Foundation of Manitoba

1031 Portage Avenue
Winnipeg, Manitoba R3G 0R8
204-944-6277
http://www.mbnet.mb.ca/crm/health/afm.html

Addiction Research Foundation (ARF)

33 Russell Street
Toronto, Ontario M5S 2S1
416-595-6100
800-463-6273 in Ontario

Alberta Alcohol and Drug Abuse Commission

10909 Jasper Avenue, 6th Floor
Edmonton, Alberta T5J 3M9
http://www.gov.ab.ca/aadac/

British Columbia Prevention Resource Centre

96 East Broadway, Suite 211
Vancouver, British Columbia V5T 1V6
604-874-8452
800-663-1880 in British Columbia

Canadian Centre on Substance Abuse

75 Albert Street, Suite 300
Ottawa, Ontario K1P 5E7
613-235-4048
http://www.ccsa.ca/

Ontario Healthy Communities Central Office

180 Dundas Street West, Suite 1900
Toronto, Ontario M5G 1Z8
416-408-4841
http://www.opc.on.ca/ohcc/

Saskatchewan Health Resource Centre

T.C. Douglas Building
3475 Albert Street
Regina, Saskatchewan S4S 6X6
306-787-3090

Websites

Avery Smartcat's Facts & Research on Children Facing Drugs
http://www.averysmartcat.com/druginfo.htm

D.A.R.E. (Drug Abuse Resistance Education) for Kids
http://www.dare-america.com/index2.htm

Elks Drug Awareness Resource Center
http://www.elks.org/drugs/

Join Together Online
http://www.jointogether.org/sa/

National Institute on Drug Abuse (NIDA)
http://www.nida.nih.gov

Partnership for a Drug-Free America
http://www.drugfreeamerica.org/

Reality Check
http://www.health.org/reality/

Substance Abuse and Mental Health Services Administration (SAMHSA)
http://www.samhsa.gov

U.S. Department of Education Safe and Drug-Free Schools Program
http://inet.ed.gov/offices/OESE/SDFS

YOU CAN'T AFFORD IT

Despite what you may have heard,
selling illegal drugs will not make you rich.

In 1998, two professors, Steven Levitt from the University of Chicago and Sudhir Venkatesh from Harvard University, released a study of how drug gangs make and distribute money. To get accurate information, Venkatesh actually lived with a drug gang in a midwestern city.

You may be surprised to find out that the average street dealer makes just about $3 an hour. You'd make more money working at McDonald's! Still think drug-dealing is a cool way to make money? What other after-school jobs carry the risk of going to prison or dying in the street from a gunshot wound?

Drug-dealing is illegal, and it kills people. If you're thinking of selling drugs or you know someone who is, ask yourself this question: is $3 an hour worth dying for or being imprisoned?

WHAT A DRUG GANG MAKES IN A MONTH*

	During a Gang War	No Gang War
INCOME (money coming in)	$ 44,500	$ 58,900
Other income (including dues and blackmail money)	10,000	18,000
TOTAL INCOME	**$ 54,500**	**$ 76,900**
EXPENSES (money paid out)		
Cost of drugs sold	$ 11,300	$ 12,800
Wages for officers and street pushers	25,600	37,600
Weapons	3,000	1,600
Tributes (fees) paid to central gang	5,800	5,900
Funeral expenses	2,300	800
Other expenses	8,000	3,400
TOTAL EXPENSES	**$ 56,000**	**$ 62,100**
TOTAL INCOME	$ 54,500	$ 76,900
MINUS TOTAL EXPENSES	- 56,000	- 62,100
TOTAL AMOUNT OF PROFIT IN ONE MONTH	**- 1,500**	**14,800**

* adapted from "Greedy Bosses," *Forbes,* August 24, 1998, p. 53.
Source: Levitt and Venkatesh.

INDEX

Picture Credits

KRISTINE BRENNAN is a writer and editor in the Philadelphia area, where she lives with her husband and son. She holds a B.A. in English with a concentration in professional writing from Elizabethtown College. This is her third book for Chelsea House.

BARRY R. McCAFFREY is Director of the Office of National Drug Control Policy (ONDCP) at the White House and a member of President Bill Clinton's cabinet. Before taking this job, General McCaffrey was an officer in the U.S. Army. He led the famous "left hook" maneuver of Operation Desert Storm that helped the United States win the Persian Gulf War.

STEVEN L. JAFFE, M.D., received his psychiatry training at Harvard University and the Massachusetts Mental Health Center and his child psychiatry training at Emory University. He has been editor of the *Newsletter of the American Academy of Child and Adolescent Psychiatry* and chairman of the Continuing Education Committee of the Georgia Psychiatric Physicians' Association. Dr. Jaffe is professor of child and adolescent psychiatry at Emory University. He is also clinical professor of psychiatry at Morehouse School of Medicine, and the director of Adolescent Substance Abuse Programs at Charter Peachford Hospital in Atlanta, Georgia.